SOMEONE I KNOW HAS MULTIPLE PERSONALITIES

A BOOK FOR SIGNIFICANT OTHERS: FRIENDS, FAMILY, AND CARING PROFESSIONALS

BY SANDRA J. HOCKING

Printed in the United States of America

01 00 99 98 97 96 95 94   5 4 3 2 1

Library of Congress Cataloging-in-publicaton Data

Hocking, Sandra J., 1948-

    Someone I know has multiple personalities : a book for significant others-- friends, family, and caring professionals / by Sandra J. Hocking.

       p.   cm.

   ISBN 1-877872-08-3 : $7.00

   1. Multiple personality—Popular works. I. Title.

RC569.5.M8H633 1994   94-11538

616.85'236—dc20   CIP

TABLE OF CONTENTS

TABLE OF CONTENTS iii

INTRODUCTION v

WHAT IS MULTIPLICITY? 1

SIGNS AND SYMPTOMS OF MULTIPLICITY 3

THE CAUSES OF MULTIPLICITY 7

WHO ARE THE PERPETRATORS? 9

DISSOCIATION 12

THE ALTERS 14

FRAGMENTS 16

MUSICAL ALTERS 17

ANIMAL ALTERS AND INANIMATE ALTERS 18

CROSS–GENDER AND CROSS–COLOR ALTERS . . . 19

CHILD ALTERS 20

ADOLESCENT ALTERS 21

ADULT ALTERS AND FULL-FLEDGED PERSONALITIES . 22

CORE PERSONALITY 23

LOSING TIME 24

SWITCHING 26

IS THE MULTIPLE DANGEROUS? 28

ANXIETY, PANIC ATTACKS AND DEPRESSION 30

SLEEPING 32

EATING DISORDERS 35

SEX 37

HEADACHES AND OTHER BODY PAINS 39

THERAPY 41

PRIVACY IS PRECIOUS. 44

MONEY 45

MEMORIES 47

MULTIPLES AS PARENTS AND CAREGIVERS 49

CHILDREN AS MULTIPLES 52

MULTIPLES AS PATIENTS 55

MULTIPLES AT SCHOOL 59

MULTIPLES AS EMPLOYEES AND COWORKERS . . . 63

MULTIPLES AS EMPLOYERS 66

RITUAL AND CULT ABUSE 68

TAKING CARE OF YOURSELF 74

SPEAKING FOR THEMSELVES 76

INTRODUCTION

Someone you know has multiple personalities, and you have lots of questions.

Many books on the market address this condition: survivor's stories, clinical literature, newsletters, magazines, and even a survival manual for multiples.

Until now, no book has existed for you—the partner, family member, friend, employer, employee, coworker, or care giver. You are known as "significant others", and you are a vital part of a multiple's healing.

You care. You want to understand and help but don't know how. The clinical literature can be daunting, and survivor's stories don't always speak to your experience.

This book, as an introduction and overview, will help answer your questions but is not meant as a diagnostic tool. (It is assumed that the person you know has already been diagnosed as having a dissociative condition.) Instead, this book gives practical advice on dealing with specific situations and on how to take care of yourself. Until recently most people believed the condition known as Multiple Personality Disorder was extremely rare. Multiples were people who wrote graphic books and appeared on talk shows. Television and movies depicted multiples as serial killers or erratic loonies unable to care for themselves.

The multiple you know probably isn't like that at all.

As more and more multiples share knowledge of their condition with significant others, this creative defense is losing some of its stigma and the fears attached to it. This is a wonderful thing! Multiples are not crazy and they aren't sick. Multiples developed alternate personalities, called alters, to survive horrendous childhood abuse. These alters kept a small child alive and sane.

For significant others it may be difficult to understand how someone can exist with so many personalities living in one body. For multiples, it may seem impossible to function with only one!

You may not know how to react or what to say. You may feel confused, frightened, helpless, frustrated, or even angry. These reactions are not unusual for anyone faced with a new situation.

This book is designed to help you understand multiplicity, not treat it. It isn't meant for therapists, though many may benefit from it. This book is meant for you, a multiple's significant other.

But first, a word about me: I wrote a book for multiples called *Living With Your Selves: A Survival Manual For People With Multiple Personalities*. I am self-employed as an author, educator, consultant, certified massage therapist and international peace advocate.

I speak frequently at child abuse conferences and train employees of women's shelters and law enforcement agencies regarding child abuse, sexual assault, ritual abuse, and multiple personality issues.

I was a multiple personality with 37 alters living in this body. Now I'm integrated and living a full and happy life. I am proof that this condition is not hopeless.

As a former multiple I'm aware of how frightening this condition can be, both inside and outside, and understand how hard it was to live and work with me. I was a difficult patient, confusing to live with, and often an unpredictable friend.

I imagine the multiple you know is something like that.

I applaud your courage in taking the time to investigate this condition for yourself. Knowing, loving, or working with a multiple may not be easy, but in the long run, you'll learn more than you expected. You'll learn about yourself, too.

Sandra J. Hocking

WHAT IS MULTIPLICITY?

Dissociative Identity Disorder, more popularly known as Multiple Personality Disorder, is the current clinical name for a psychiatric condition in which two or more personalities inhabit the same body. These personalities may "take over" the body, or "come out," and often exhibit behavior that is out of character for the "host," or main personality.

It is NOT demonic possesion!

Except for insurance purposes, the word "disorder" is falling out of favor with both multiples and therapists. Rather than a disorder, this condition is being recognized as a highly creative defense mechanism. So for the rest of this book, I will refer to this condition as multiple personalities or multiplicity.

You may also hear it called MPD, Multiple Personality Gift, Multiple Personality Response, or Multiple Personality Defense.

The analogy I used in my previous book, *Living With Your Selves*, is this: Imagine that the multiple's system is like a bus, with the host as the bus itself. Inside, alters are sleeping, reading, playing, or looking out different windows. Occasionally an alter may sit in the driver's seat and direct where the bus goes and what it does—often without the host's knowledge or consent.

Multiplicity occurs on a continuum. Multiples on the milder end of the scale may only hear voices, and time loss may be infrequent. These multiples often hold responsible jobs, raise families, and function well in society.

Multiples at the other end of the scale may be truly dysfunctional, with alters switching at will, and no contact between the selves. These multiples may revolve through the hospital or prison system, experience severe time loss, and have extreme difficulty coping with daily life.

Most multiples are somewhere in between.

SIGNS AND SYMPTOMS OF MULTIPLICITY

Even though this book is not designed to be used to diagnose the condition of multiplicity, it might be helpful here to list some of the signs and symptoms of multiple personalities. Remember that not all multiples are alike, and not all symptoms apply to all multiples, so this list is understandably not all inclusive:

Physical

- Changes in voice—male, female, childlike

- Changes in facial expression or structure

- Changes in body posture, language, gestures

- Change in handedness (one alter may be left-handed, another may be right-handed)

- Unexplained eating disorders

- Major discrepancy in clothing, makeup (female multiples are often more comfortable in pants because of the presence of male alters)

Behavioral

- Changes in voice—quality, accent, vocabulary

- Differences in talent (for example, one alter may paint or draw, another write or sing, while others don't have the same ability)

- Changes in handwriting

- Time loss or distortion

- Memory loss or distortion

- Unexplained phobias

- Anxiety and panic attacks

- May be perceived as "pathological liars"

- Hears voices inside the head, sometimes as a "word salad" or as entire conversations

- May speak of "thinking somebody else's thoughts" or of living "parallel lives"

- Refers to self in the third person, using the pronouns we, she, or he, instead of "I" when speaking of themselves

- Easily hypnotized

- Self-mutilates, sometimes with no memory of the event

- History of suicide attempts

- May not recognize persons with whom she/he has a relationship

- Great changes in food likes/dislikes

Physiologic symptoms

- Headaches

- Unpredictable response to medication

- Changes in tolerance to pain

- Extraordinarily rapid healing

- Paralysis, blindness, or illness in one alter but not in others

- Changes in blood pressure, blood type, and medical test results

Substance abuse

- Alcohol

- Drugs

- Rarely, hallucinogens

Sexual behavior

- Acting out (promiscuity one day, total abstinence the next)

- "Deviant" behavior such as bestiality or sadomasochism

A common misconception is that everybody is multiple to some degree. Although everyone has different aspects to their personality, not everyone suffers from multiple personalities.

Creating alternate personalities in response to trauma is not the same thing as the normal imaginary friend that most children have in childhood. An imaginary friend doesn't change behavior or cause memory loss. Kids know an imaginary friend is only pretend. However, multiples often do not know the alters exist, or are perceived as people unrelated to themselves.

For example, you may act differently at work than you do at home. You behave differently on the baseball diamond than when you make love to your partner. The key here is that you are always the one performing these activities, and you are likely to remember doing them. You know you played baseball after work yesterday. You remember making love with your partner last night. A multiple may not.

Creating different personalities in response to trauma is not the same thing as having different aspects to the same personality. Depending on how severe their dissociation, multiples may not remember from one day to the next what another alter did. A multiple friend of mine put it this way, "A singleton forgets to take out the trash. A multiple doesn't know where the trash is or even that it belongs to her!"

For a Multiple Personality Disorder and Ritual Abuse Help List, contact:

VOICES in Action, Inc.
P.O. Box 148309
Chicago, IL 60614
(312) 327-1500

THE CAUSES OF MULTIPLICITY

Multiple personalities are caused by severe and repeated childhood abuse, generally beginning before the age of five. Clinical literature suggests that over 95% of this abuse is sexual. Other causes may stem from physical or emotional abuse, ritual abuse or neglect.

Sexual abuse may include intercourse, sodomy, oral sex, being touched in a sexual manner or forced to watch such acts, mutual masturbation, pornography, and bestiality. Some sexual abuse does not involve physical contact at all, but may take the form of being watched during bathing, dressing, or going to the toilet, and never having the privacy to do private things.

Physical abuse may result in bruises, broken bones, black eyes, and injury to the point of death. These children may have been pushed down stairs, burned with cigarettes or hot water, had their hair pulled out or their faces slapped. They may have been beaten with fists, whips, coat hangers, electrical cords, wooden spoons, tree switches, or clubs.

Children or adults who have been physically abused may be hypervigilant to their surroundings, always on the lookout for danger. These people may flinch at sudden movements or cringe when spoken to harshly. Multiples may switch to another personality instantly if the system feels threatened.

Emotional abuse is more nebulous and more difficult to stop. Constant criticisms, name calling, being called "stupid," and told "I wish you'd never been born," are common. Constantly ridiculing the child's fears and being told to "shut up!" when crying can ruin a child's fragile self-esteem. Emotional abuse is as damaging as a fist.

Child Protective Service agencies are often helpless in the face of emotional abuse. In some ways it's easier to intervene if the child is being physically or sexually abused.

Neglected children may not be fed or clothed appropriately. They may be locked in closets, basements, or even cages. These children may be starved for long periods of time. If allowed to go to school, they often fall asleep in class for lack of nourishment and may be grossly underweight. They may be left home alone for extended periods. Neglected children often have a haunted, tired look.

Unlike children living in poverty, whose parents can't care for them, neglected children's parents won't care for them. Sometimes the neglect is rationalized as punishment for some minor infraction of household rules.

We will discuss ritual abuse in some detail later in this book.

I found these books to be helpful in understanding child abuse:

The Courage To Heal, A Guide For Women Survivors Of Child Sexual Abuse
by Ellen Bass and Laura Davis

Child Abuse Prevention Handbook
available from:
Crime Prevention Center
Office of the Attorney General
P.O. Box 944255
Sacramento, CA 94244-2550

WHO ARE THE PERPETRATORS?

Now that we've discussed what multiplicity is and its causes, let's talk about those who commit the abuses that produce it.

Abuse is most often perpetrated by a primary caretaker such as mother, father, sibling, or baby-sitter. Other abusers may include family friends or relatives, teachers, ministers, or anyone who has access to the child.Child molesters come in many types. The pedophile is a person whose sexual preference is children. Often these people have a preference for a certain sex or age of child. This person may seek out jobs that require contact with children or volunteer as coaches or youth group leaders.

Pedophiles actually believe that they are not harming children by having sex with them. They may believe they are initiating the child into adulthood, or that sex between adults and children is natural. They often quote lore from other cultures that encourage the father to be a girl child's first sexual partner.

Pedophiles may belong to organizations that encourage adult/child sexual activity.

Most child molesters are opportunistic offenders. This person may have an ongoing sexual relationship with another adult but will abuse children when or if circumstances permit.

The opportunistic offender may not even be planning to abuse a child. Giving the child a bath, dressing the child, or even playing "tickle," can provide an opportunity for the offender to abuse a child. It only takes a second for someone to slip a hand into a child's panties and destroy trust and love forever.

Opportunistic offenders may feel shame and revulsion for what they have done. In some cases the first time may be the only time. More often the first time is only the beginning.

Offenders may rationalize their behavior by saying that the child was being seductive, the abuse was the child's fault, or that the child was being punished or rewarded.

Alcohol and drugs are sometimes used as an excuse. People who profess that drugs or alcohol are the reason for their behavior are only kidding themselves. Substance abuse does not create a child molester; it only makes it easier for molesters to justify their actions to themselves or to society.

Women, contrary to popular belief, do indeed abuse children. Usually these women were themselves abused and are acting out the circumstances of their own childhoods.

Sometimes children abuse other children. A brother or sister, baby-sitter, or bully may use sexual abuse as methods of power and control. I'm not discussing normal sexual exploration here, but the sexual exploitation and humiliation of one child by another.

Perpetrators do not just disappear when their victims reach adulthood. Often they remain a part of the multiple's life. It may be difficult for you, as a significant other, to understand this ongoing relationship.

You need to remember that not all members of a multiple's system see this person as an abuser. Some may remember only the good portions of the relationship. Others who recall the abuse may have different levels of interaction with the abuser. And some may still be seeking the love, protection, and approval they never received as a child.

If possible, ascertain whether or not the abuse is still occurring. It is not unheard of for the abuse to continue even after the victim has married or has moved away from home.

Many significant others want to exact some sort of revenge for the damage done to the person she/he cares about. I understand how tempting it can be to want to resort to physical violence. However, it will do the multiple no good if you end up in jail. So keep a cool head and trust that the issue of an ongoing relationship with the abuser will be addressed in therapy.

If the multiple you know is still in danger, you may need to help extricate them from the situation immediately. Never leave a child alone with abusers. It may be necessary to enlist the help of proper authorities to remove the child from dangerous situations, such as home or preschool.

If the multiple is an adult, you may need to gain the cooperation of the entire system in order to limit access to the abusers. For help and suggestions, be sure to talk with the multiple as well as his or her therapist.

For more information on perpetrators, read:

Why They Did It
by O'Brien, and published by Charles Thomas
or contact:
Safer Society Program
P.O. Box 340
Brandon, VT 05733
Phone: (802) 247-3132

DISSOCIATION

A small child does not have the same capacity for emotional defense as an adult. If an adult is being hurt or abused, she/he can fight back, either verbally or physically. Unable to fight against perpetrators stronger and more powerful, something called dissociation is a child's only defense.

The dictionary defines dissociation as "the act of separating or state of being separated." In psychological terms this means that persons mentally distance themselves from traumatic situations or emotional distress. People also dissociate when they are bored or performing routine tasks.

With dissociation, children can mentally remove themselves from terrifying or dangerous situations. Dissociation creates a safe place in a child's mind. It may feel to the child as if she/he is floating on the ceiling, or has gone to a favorite safe room or outside to play in the park.

Everybody dissociates. Highway hypnosis, or distracted inattention, are common forms of dissociation. Making a grocery list in your head while listening to a boring lecture is one example of dissociation, as is spacing out during an argument.

Children who dissociate during abuse may create other children in their minds who are more capable of dealing with the abuse. These alternate children take on a life of their own and come out to handle various situations. Once this defense is in place, it is easy to create other alters, and still others as the abuse continues.

Dissociation in and of itself is not a bad thing. Everybody does it, and it is a valuable tool for a child with no other defense. In childhood, dissociating out of abusive situations was necessary. It is only in adulthood, if the abuse has stopped, that dissociation becomes a problem, as it is no longer needed as a survival skill. If the abuse is still continuing into adulthood, then dissociation and the creation of alternate personalities may still be useful as a defense.

Dissociation to the point of creating multiple personalities is a healthy response to an unhealthy situation, a sane internal response to external insanity.

At a lecture I attended recently, Dr. Colin Ross put it this way: "Multiple Personality Disorder is a normal thing to have if you have suffered severe childhood abuse."

For more information on multiple personalities and on incest, write:

Lear's magazine
655 Madison Avenue
New York, NY 10021
and ask for the February 1992 issue.

THE ALTERS

Alternate personalities, called alters, are created in response to trauma and can be of any age and of many ages. They may be the opposite gender from the host or have different sexual orientations. There may be as few as three or as many as hundreds.

Multiples may refer to their alters as a system by using such terms as "my friends," "my inside kids," or "the committee."

Alters come in many shapes and sizes including fragments, full-fledged personalities, animal and inanimate alters, gatekeepers, and internal self-helpers. Not all alters have names. It is quite common for alters simply to be called by their function or basic personality trait, such as The Destroyer, The Whore, The One Who Knows, or The Sad One.

New alters may be created into adulthood as seemingly threatening situations arise. For example, when I was 40 years old, I got a job as client services coordinator with a women's refuge. This job entailed counseling victims of sexual assault and domestic violence, public speaking, and facilitating support groups.

Because I was unsure of myself in this position, I created two new alters to handle the situation, Roberta and Kate. Now that I'm integrated, I find that the talents and attributes of these alters are a part of my own personality.

Sometimes the alters know about each other and sometimes not. Part of therapy is getting the entire system to know and accept one another and function as a cohesive and cooperative unit. Until that happens, though, a great portion of the host's life may be lost to the alters.

It is important to remember that not all multiples are alike! Just as no two human beings have the exact same experiences in life, no two multiples do either. Not only does each multiple have a different history, so does each alter within a multiple's system.

One alter, for example, may remember only the good things about the abuser: the trips to the circus, building a birdhouse in the backyard, or sharing a bedtime story.

Another alter may remember the abuse perpetrated by this same person and be unable to understand how the other alter can love the very person who abused them.

FRAGMENTS

Although many alters are full-fledged personalities, others are designed only to carry certain memories, handle specific emotions, or deal with very definite situations. These alters are called fragments.

For example, if a child is yelled at and hit every time she/he does the dishes, a specific alter fragment may be created only to wash dishes perfectly. When not washing dishes, this alter recedes into the safety of the internal system and rarely comes out at any other time.

Fragmented alters rarely make themselves known unless the particular situation they were designed to handle is present. Fragments are also the easiest to integrate when and if the time comes.

MUSICAL ALTERS

Many multiples have musical alters who are designed to keep the host busy listening to internal music in order not to remember the abuse. The music may interfere with sleeping and sometimes with carrying on a conversation. It may sound like a radio being turned on full blast inside the head or like quiet nonstop background noise.

This alter may play music during sexual acts. This keeps the inside children occupied and distant from what may seem like danger. If your partner hums during sex, this may mean that the musical alter is close to the front of the system, ready to step in at the first sign of danger.

A musical alter may either be a fragment or a full-fledged personality but is not the music itself.

ANIMAL ALTERS AND INANIMATE ALTERS

Some multiples also have animal alters (such as dragons or lions) or inanimate alters (such as trees or rocks). Animal alters are often powerful forces, designed for protection or anger. These alters may seem larger than life, rarely speak, but may make appropriate roars or growls.

Inanimate alters such as trees, rocks, or walls may appear mute, unseeing, and unfeeling. If you are being hurt, and you're three years old, it helps to have an alter who feels nothing.

CROSS–GENDER AND CROSS–COLOR ALTERS

Some white female multiples have black male alters. The black male in this case is perceived as a powerful figure, able to ward off danger and provide a sense of safety. These alters are usually valiant protectors of the system.

In addition, it is quite common to have alters who perceive themselves as a different sex than the physical body. This can sometimes cause problems, such as when a male alter in a female body chooses to use the men's room in a public place.

During therapy, as alters begin to have a more accurate perception of themselves and the others in the system, cross-gender alters may begin to question their sexuality. One of my alters, Peter, had a long discussion with my therapist as to why he didn't have a penis, when all the other boys had one. He was convinced that his penis had been damaged or would grow later.

Alters may also have a different sexual orientation than the host. Lesbian alters in a woman who is married to a man can cause great strain on a marriage, as can gay alters for a man who is married to a woman.

If these alters do not perceive themselves as being married, then why should they be faithful? This logic calls for supreme understanding on the part of the spouse or significant other in a relationship with a multiple.

CHILD ALTERS

Child alters will behave like children, because to them, that's what they are. Living in an adult body doesn't seem to matter, because they don't see the body as grown-up, anyway.

Two-year-old alters will act and talk like two-year-olds. They may be occasionally incontinent, unable to manipulate a crayon, speak a cohesive sentence, or read. Or she/he may cry or get angry and throw temper tantrums, even in public places.

A child alter may also be fun-loving and playful. She/he may hug favorite people on sight, or clap hands delightedly at a snowflake. She/he may play with the toys at K-Mart or put dozens of candy bars in the grocery basket at Safeway.

Some child alters carry a great deal of the pain for the system and may cry inconsolably, scream in terror, or huddle up into a ball with eyes tightly closed.

A child alter must be treated as a child and spoken to in terms a child understands. They need firm boundaries and lots of love. Most especially, they need a great deal of understanding, particularly when reliving traumatic memories.

Remember, these alters literally never grew up and live in perpetual childhood, often a never-never land filled with pain. They need lots of hugs, toys, dolls, crayons and stuffed animals. They also need plenty of opportunity to process the memories they hold, and a safe, supportive person to hold them when they cry, if this feels safe for them.

Child alters may be fragments or full-fledged personalities.

ADOLESCENT ALTERS

Teenage alters may be defiant, pop chewing gum, or screech rock music on the stereo. They may treat you like a parent, no matter what your relationship is in real life.

They may prefer the company of other teenagers and will take part in adolescent activities. One danger is that the adolescent alter may want to have a sexual relationship with another teenager, which could lead to charges of sexual abuse for the adult host. A teenage alter may be the life of the party at a teen gathering.

Teen alters, like any adolescent, are masters at getting into trouble. They may call people names, giggle at the slightest provocation, flip the minister "the bird," or try out their sexuality with a variety of partners. They may string paper clips together at work, or play practical jokes on coworkers.

Adolescent alters need very firm boundaries. They must not be allowed to rule the household or create havoc at work. Inappropriate behavior for real teenagers is not acceptable in teenage alters either.

It is important to allow the multiple to accept the responsibility for their own actions. Constantly bailing out an alter who gets into trouble does no more good than bailing out an alcoholic every time she/he gets put in jail for drunk driving. You must allow the multiple to accept the consequences for their behavior.

It is not your job to police the system! Just as your actions are your responsibility, a multiple's behavior belongs to the multiple. Inappropriate behavior on the part of any alter is the responsibility of that internal system.

ADULT ALTERS AND FULL-FLEDGED
PERSONALITIES

Adult alters may be protective, destructive, talented, or mute. They often have lives outside of the host's life, their own circle of friends and interests, and their own way of looking at the world. For the multiple it may feel as if they are living parallel lives, with brief and infrequent glimpses into the world of the others.

This glimpse may be frustrating for the multiple, as the peek into an alter's life may be immediately "forgotten" or blocked out.

Adults are highly individualistic and may boast talents the host does not possess. One may be able to sing or paint, while none of the others have the same ability. Some alters express the rage for the system or feel the grief.

GATEKEEPERS

Gatekeepers direct which alter goes out into the world. They may control frequency and length of body time. Gatekeepers rarely come out on their own but are content to oversee the comings and goings of everyone else.

INTERNAL SELF–HELPERS

Internal Self–Helpers (sometimes called an ISH) help to keep the system safe and are often a great help in the therapeutic process. These alters may know a great deal about the history of each alter.

CORE PERSONALITY

Most systems have a central or core personality. Sometimes this personality (often called The Original Child) is "sleeping" or may even be said to be "dead." Alters are usually quite protective of this original child and will go to great lengths to protect him or her.

For more information on multiplicity, and to hear the alters speak for themselves, this book is invaluable:

Multiple Personality Disorder From The Inside Out
Edited by Barry Cohen, Esther Giller, and Lynn W.
published by the Sidran Foundation
2328 West Joppa Road, Suite 15
Lutherville, MD 21093

The Sidran Foundation also has an excellent resource catalog.

LOSING TIME

As different alters take control of the body, others are pushed into the background and often have no knowledge of what is happening.

Multiples may suddenly find themselves in a frightening situation, in a place they don't remember going, or talking to someone they don't know. They may find evidence that an alter has been out and done something inappropriate or even destructive.

Losing time is always scary, but over the years, the multiple has learned to cover his/her anxiety. To a singleton, aside from a twitch or a pause in the conversation, and maybe an excuse as the multiple dashes away, nothing may seem amiss.

But losing time is frightening, emotionally painful, and may make the multiple extremely angry. Losing time is like losing part of yourself. It's frustrating to have no control over those who are living your life. However, losing time may also mean that the alters are simply sharing the body and not necessarily that the host became frightened or upset.

The multiple should be kept informed of his/her activities while an alter was in control, even if that alter did something embarrassing or destructive. The most frightening thing about losing time is never being sure of exactly what you did.

There are many ways to help the multiple cope with time loss. One multiple and her husband agreed to audiotape any conversations he has with his wife's alters. Another keeps notes and shares what activities occurred while the host was "away."

Don't try to keep the inappropriate behavior of an alter from the host! Multiples are very sensitive to lying in any form and will probably pick up that you aren't telling the whole truth.

You don't need to embellish the truth, act shocked, or make threats—but the host does need to know if somebody in the system is doing something illegal, immoral, or inappropriate. This needs to be done in a kind and gentle manner. Do not confront the multiple in anger, as this will only cause resentment and pain in the system.

Multiples are often afraid to ask what happened during the time that was lost. You can help by sharing as completely as possible what transpired. The host may feel uncomfortable or embarrassed, but it's significant information. Even if no untoward event occurred, it is important to share that information. For one thing, they may not even be aware they were gone!

It is entirely possible to lose time and not be aware of it. Often an alter will be out for only a moment or two to join a conversation, write a note, drink a soda, smoke a cigarette, or engage in a particular sex act. When this happens, the host may not be aware of any lost time at all.

I can remember going to my therapist and hearing him say, "About that letter you wrote." The problem was, I didn't remember writing any letter, and I didn't remember losing time.

The multiple you know may do similar things.

For more information, this is available in both book form, and on tape:

Allies In Healing, When The Person You Love Was Sexually Abused As A Child
by Laura Davis

SWITCHING

Switching involves moving from one personality state into another. Sometimes this is in response to perceived danger from the outside or from inside memories. Switching is rarely "Hollywood" style, like you see in the movies. It is usually a subtle change and not at all flamboyant. Most people perceive the switches as mood swings.

When many alters come out in a short length of time, the "revolving door" effect happens. The multiple may not be able to complete a sentence or may undergo bodily changes and twitches. This is both frustrating and frightening. Often massive headaches will occur as the body adjusts to each new alter.

How long the alters remain out depends on the situation. If the host was frightened into retreating, many alters may come out in turn, especially if the situation is truly dangerous.

In therapy, though, alters may come out only for a short time in order to work on their own issues. Sometimes they will pop out for a minute or two, often to add their "two cents worth" to a conversation. And I had alters who came out only on paper, to write or draw.

As therapy progresses and all the different parts of the self begin to know each other, there will be internal agreement as to who gets to come out and when. But in the beginning the switching may be uncontrollable. Whichever alter is best equipped to handle a certain situation, or who has been programmed to do so, will be the one to come out.

Identifying the alters is easy once you know what to look for. However, constantly asking, "Who are you now?" is not a good idea.

What usually happens is that all of a sudden everybody runs away, and nobody is left to answer the question. Or the host knows somebody is in the forefront but doesn't know who.

Except in certain circumstances, facilitating or encouraging switching is not a good idea. This only reinforces the switching behavior and makes it more difficult for the system to gain control over itself.

Some exceptions include an alter behaving in a self-destructive or outwardly destructive manner; an alter acting inappropriately at work or some social function; or a child alter is out and an adult alter needs to drive home.

If you do need to ask for a switch of personalities, be sure to reassure the alter currently in control that she/he is not bad, but that someone else needs to come out now; ask for a calm, rational adult personality. You may need to explain to the system why a switch is necessary; and suggest to the alter who is going inside that she/he can come out again at a more appropriate time.

Be sure to keep your word! Trust is a fragile commodity for a multiple.

You may find you need to attend a support group specifically for the significant others of multiples or other survivors of childhood trauma. Al-Anon meetings may also be helpful, as the people who go to these meetings are familiar with the irrational behavior of people they care about. These meetings can be helpful in venting your fears, frustrations, and confusion and help you to understand your part in the healing process.

IS THE MULTIPLE DANGEROUS?

Movies and books make it seem as if every multiple has an alter who is a serial killer. Well, that's just not true. In the overwhelming majority of cases, if a multiple is dangerous, it's to themselves and not others. If the person you know was not an ax murderer before the diagnosis was made, it's unlikely she/he will become one afterwards. We're not talking Dr. Jekyll and Mr. Hyde here.

Multiplicity is a defense mechanism that was designed to keep the system safe, not put it in danger. However, some multiples do have alters who may indeed be destructive to their own system, and more rarely to others. This alter may be suicidal or may injure the body in some way. Although this may make no sense to you, it may make perfect sense to them.

Self-injurious behavior is triggered by many things. Sometimes the urges are in response to outside events but may also be internal. Injuring the body may be a sign of severe internal emotional distress. Cutting or burning the body may actually seem like a way to stay in control of a frightening situation. If a multiple is concentrating on outside pain, then she/he doesn't have to focus on the inside pain.

One of the ways that molesters keep their victims silent is by such threats as, "If you tell, I'll kill you." As the multiple begins to remember the abuse and to talk about it, these underlying messages may trigger the subconscious mind into self-destructive behavior.

Unless you are an abuser yourself, who deliberately fuels these urges, you are not responsible for the multiple's self-destructive behavior! This is strictly the responsibility of the multiple.

You can help by simply being there. Provide as much of a safe environment as you can. Identifying which alter is suicidal or destructive can often help diffuse the situation. It helps to understand that the alter who is destructive is acting out a tremendous amount of internal pain. A little understanding goes a long way.

Of course you can't, and shouldn't provide twenty-four-hour-a-day supervision. If some part of a multiple's system is determined to injure the body, it will be done without your knowledge anyway. Don't blame yourself if this occurs.

If the multiple you know is self-destructive, it is important to provide as much support and understanding as you can. Ask how you can help by getting suggestions from the multiple and the multiple's therapist. Give them time to go to therapy regularly—it's important—and don't gripe about the cost.

Most multiples would be horrified at the thought of hurting anyone the way they've been hurt, but some do have alters who may be perpetrators. If this is the case, extreme care must be taken to protect your outside children, if you have any.

It is important to make an agreement with the alters that "Nobody hurts the kids!" and ask for a nonoffending alter to be vigilant if a perpetrating alter is out.

An excellent little book for those just beginning to understand multiplicity is:

Multiple Personality, An Outcome of Child Abuse
by Margo Rivera, Ph.D.

ANXIETY, PANIC ATTACKS AND DEPRESSION

Many multiples suffer from severe anxiety and panic attacks or have bouts of depression. These incidents may be triggered at the slightest provocation and often occur without warning. The scent of an aftershave in a grocery store, the sight of a crying child, or the barking of a dog can cause a reaction.

Crying and feelings of terror are common. She/he may try to hide in the closet or under furniture. She/he may curl up into the fetal position, or rock back and forth rhythmically. She/he may freeze and be unable to move, speak, or tell you what the problem is.

Anxiety and panic attacks may be caused by emerging memories or flashbacks. The already hazy line between *now* and *then* may virtually disappear, and the abuse feels as though it is taking place right now, at the present time, all over again.

Depression may last for days and may become so severe that the multiple cannot even get out of bed. Life doesn't seem worth living, and the multiple may stop eating or attending to normal hygiene routines. In such instances, calling on professional help is a must. Don't try to handle this alone.

Sometimes contributing factors include the consumption of certain foods or drinks such as caffeine, sugar, chocolate, and alcohol. Reducing the intake of these substances can sometimes help limit the frequency of anxiety, panic attacks, and depression.

Soft music, relaxation tapes, low lights, and fragrant, pretty flowers may help to lessen the fear. Reminding the multiple to breathe reduces the anxiety. Help to ground the multiple in reality by talking in a low, quiet, calm voice but do not speak in a monotone.

Becoming angry or frightened yourself only worsens the situation. Remind the multiple that the abuse is not happening now. Now, he or she is safe. Now, it's going to be okay.

Sometimes you may simply have to let the attack run its course. As always, previous preparation is a plus in these situations. Find out from the multiple and the therapist just what role you should play, if any. It could be that the best course of action is for you to leave the multiple to work out the fears alone.

This video is helpful to survivors and significant others:

Healing Sexual Abuse, The Recovery Process
hosted by Dr. Eliana Gil
1-800-621-9167

SLEEPING

Sleep disturbances are common for multiples. Often memories surface in the dream state and may be perceived as nightmares. The multiple may fight off going to sleep for fear of reliving these memories.

Dreams may also be symbolic. Someone who dreams of burying a body, for example, may subconsciously be recreating the suppression of memories. The multiple may dream of people who have died or people who don't exist. Alters may interject themselves into a dream to relay a message or place a memory into the conscious mind.

Nightmares are terrifying dreams and the person may wake up screaming. The person will usually be able to relate the dream, and may feel disoriented and frightened for a few minutes after.

Night terrors may also wake the person up, but often she/he may not know what was so frightening. Shaking, crying or screaming may accompany night terrors.

Multiples may become so frightened by nightmares or night terrors that they may refuse to go to sleep. Insomnia is common. They may clean house, write, sew, work on the car, or do almost anything to avoid going to sleep and facing their dreams once more.

Musical alters are often most active at night. They attempt to keep the dreams and memories away by playing music. The problem is that they also may keep the multiple from resting.

Escape sleeping is also quite common for multiples, and sometimes for singletons, too. The escape sleeper is one who goes to sleep in order to escape memories or difficult situations. Escape sleepers may sleep ten or twelve hours a night and take a nap in the afternoon as well. They may be lethargic and overweight.

Some multiples may sleep in one position only, such as on their backs or with their backs to the wall. Some would rather sleep on the side closest to the door. Some multiples insist on having all doors, including the closet, open. Others don't feel safe unless all doors are closed and locked.

When feeling particularly threatened, some multiples may retreat to a place that reminds them of a safe place they had when a child. I have heard of multiples who sleep in the closet on the shoes, down in the basement under the stairs, or even in the bathtub, with the door locked.

Many multiples sleep with a stuffed animal a teddy bear or with a favorite doll. They may sleep with the radio on, or a tape that turns itself over. One multiple I know has a night light plugged into every available outlet. They may be hypervigilant to the point of waking at every creak of the house or at unexpected noise.

For many multiples, nighttime was never a time of safety. Abusers often came under the cover of darkness, so it is no surprise that multiples attempt to feel safe in any way they can. Some multiples even take night jobs, because the only time they can truly rest is during the day.

If the abuse occurred about the same time every night, then the multiple may wake up at that time, even without provocation or current threat.

Don't make jokes about whatever methods the multiple uses to feel safe or be hurt because somehow your presence is not enough. The multiple is working through many years of pain, and as much as you would like to be the stable rock in their lives, sometimes you may not be enough.

These books are must reading for significant others:

Outgrowing the Pain, A Book For And About Adults Abused As Children

Outgrowing The Pain Together, A Book For Spouses And Partners Of Adults Abused As Children.
Both are by Dr. Eliana Gil.

EATING DISORDERS

Many multiples, or alters within the system, have a problem with food. She/he may be a compulsive overeater, anorexic, bulimic (or both!), or have severe phobias about certain foods.

Different alters may have different problems. An alter who eats compulsively and another who is anorexic or bulimic may war with each other constantly over the amount of food the body requires to function.

Roller-coaster dieting is common, as is constant frustration about weight or body image. Multiples often have no concept of their own body size. A child alter looks in the mirror and sees a child. An overweight alter looks in the mirror and sees rolls of fat, even if the reality of the body is quite thin.

One personality may go to the gym and work out for hours, switch on the way home, and a different alter gorge herself at the next ice-cream parlor or donut shop.

Why Food?

Well, for many multiples, food was the only thing she/he could control as a child. If she/he was forced to have oral sex at the age of five or six or twelve, it is easy to make the subconscious decision not to put anything in his/her mouth that doesn't taste terrific. Multiples may become addicted to sugar, chocolate, and diet soda.

The consumption or avoidance of food may be a form of rebellion against the abusers. Like a two-year-old that stamps a tiny foot and says, "I don't have to eat it, and you can't make me!" eating or not eating is an attempt to control at least one thing in their lives.

Eating may be a solitary affair, something done in secret. Overeaters hide candy bars in the laundry basket or eat boxes of cookies in the car. There seems to be a subconscious brain-burp that says, "If nobody sees me eat it, then it didn't really happen."

Bulimics, on the other hand, take the other extreme. They may eat in front of you, only to vomit the offending food later. Once again, if the act wasn't witnessed, then it didn't really happen.

Consider that if the only revenge a person has against those hurting them is body size or the overindulgence or avoidance of food, then they'll take that revenge. Conversely, if the only positive attention a person gets is due to being slim, or from being a member of the Clean Plate Club, then that behavior is reinforced, even if it is no longer appropriate.

Eating disorders are a complicated issue, one not fully understood even by the clinical community. Of course, having an eating disorder does not extrapolate into multiplicity. But it does complicate matters tremendously.

For more information on eating disorders and a possible solution, this book may be helpful:

The Food Fix, A Recovery Guide For Destructive Eaters
by Sandra Gordon Stoltz

SEX

For many multiples and their partners, sex can be one of the most difficult areas of life. It may cause almost as many arguments as money and certainly causes as much pain.

If you are the partner of a multiple, you need to keep in mind that sex takes on a whole new meaning. Not everyone in the system may be in a relationship with you. Some alters may have a different sexual orientation or perceive themselves as a different gender than the physical body.

Child personalities who have been programmed to believe that all they are good for is sex may come out during lovemaking. Or your partner may simply seem to slip away in the middle of passion, leaving an alter behind who wants no part of the proceedings.

Sometimes certain sexual acts or locations will trigger a switch of personalities. Oral sex or sodomy will certainly bring out the alter who is best equipped to deal with these activities.

Gentle and loving sex may seem scary, especially if the original abuse was clothed in kind words and tender touches.

Your partner may suddenly freeze up or become unresponsive. You may sense a different quality to the lovemaking. A gentle encounter may turn perverse or even feel cruel and nasty.

Before making love, you may need to make an agreement with your partner and his or her alters. Arrange with adult alters to keep the kids inside and safe. Even though it may take a little of the edge off your lovemaking, you must keep a vigilant watch over switches. Sometimes the slightest thing will trigger a reaction.

If a switch occurs during sex, it is very important that you ascertain who the "new" person is. If the alter who came out is a child, you must stop immediately. For these children, sex is seen as a punishment, fraught with danger and pain. Even though the body in front of you is adult, the emotions and feelings are those of a child.

Sex with multiples can be a complicated issue. It is best to work out the details of your sex life with the multiple, the alters, and the therapist.

While the prospect of making love to many people in one body may seem exciting, it's damaging to encourage switching for this purpose. And remember that any alter in the multiple's system has the right to say no.

For more help in understanding and healing your current sex life, this book may be helpful:

Ghosts In The Bedroom, A Guide For Partners Of Incest Survivors
by Ken Graber, M.A.

HEADACHES AND OTHER BODY PAINS

For many multiples, headaches are an ongoing problem. Sometimes these headaches can be of migraine intensity, especially when alters revolve through the system at will. Other multiples will have a headache every time a switch occurs.

In some cases the headache is in response to a memory or may itself be a body memory. A body memory happens when the body remembers the details of the abuse, even when the mind doesn't.

Sometimes it helps to experiment with different "cures" for the headache. Medication may or may not help, as each alter reacts to medication in different ways. Also, the alter who takes the medication may not be the one who sticks around to see if it works.

Some people use cold packs on the back of the neck, others take a hot bath. Some find music soothing, others lay down in a darkened room. Some multiples find a back and neck massage soothing. A cup of hot chamomile or peppermint tea or the scent of lavender or rose may be just the ticket to diffuse a headache.

A little trick I learned in massage therapy school is to hold one finger over the site of the worst part of the pain, and concentrate all the pain in that spot. Then take the finger away and imagine the pain pouring out until it's all gone.

It's important to remember that not every headache is a body memory or a sign of switching. Some headaches are just headaches like everybody gets once in a while.

In addition to headaches, the body may show the effects of the abuse through body aches, sore throats, stomachaches, rashes or bruises, or even temporary blindness. Broken bones may appear only on the X-ray of the personality who sustained the injury. Many women have severe cramps monthly or experience pelvic floor or rectal pain for no apparent reason.

As with other physical ailments, one alter may experience a physical discomfort, and others in the system won't. Alters who drink to excess may leave another alter with the hangover. An alter who has surgery may leave another personality to convalesce.

Significant others often feel helpless in the face of body memories or unexplained pain and illness. Sometimes the only thing you can do is remain supportive and comforting. Once again, this is an issue that needs to be resolved with the multiple's system and therapist.

Another book you may find helpful is:

Family Fallout, A Handbook For Families Of Adult Sexual Abuse Survivors
by Dorothy Beaulieu Landry

THERAPY

Therapy is an important part of healing for many multiples. In addition to traditional "sit and talk" therapy, other methods may be helpful in working with multiples.

Group therapy may provide feelings of belonging and invaluable support. Groups should be facilitated by a licensed therapist. Although self-run groups may seem valuable, they can create confusion and self-doubt for all members of the group.

As I look back on it now, I believe that the groups I attended, even though I thought they were helpful at the time, actually slowed down my progress. My focus was more on their stuff than my stuff, which was a great way to repress the work that I needed to do.

You see, when your own memories are few, it is tempting to "try on" someone else's. Sort of like a shoe, if the memory fits, it's yours. If it doesn't, you'll discard it. The burden of carrying around someone else's trauma while you decide if it belongs to you can be staggering. The multiple you know may spend a great deal of time trying to figure out exactly what their own reality is.

Even hearing the memories of other people can be traumatic. It is important that trained counselors facilitate this process, and help the multiple cope not only with their own memories but with those of others.

It seems appropriate to talk for a moment about "false" memories. A current theory among some people and professionals, called False Memory Syndrome, is that memories can be implanted into a client by the therapist, creating memories of abuse that never happened.

It's a tempting and seductive theory. All multiples and all survivors of childhood trauma want desperately to believe that none of their memories of abuse are true. The proponents of False Memory Syndrome provide the multiple or survivor an easy way out.

While this may occasionally occur, such cases are extremely rare and certainly do not happen to the extent the False Memory Syndrome Foundation would have you believe.

Most multiples went into therapy because of their memories. Survivors of childhood abuse tend to doubt their memories because the events being recalled are so traumatic. Denial is built right in to the healing process.

Memories that are remembered on the multiple's own time, so to speak, can usually be believed. But memories recovered in a therapist's office, in group, or under hypnosis can also be believed.

Most therapists know enough about their job not to implant any ideas into a client. It's important that a person remembers their own truth, in their own way, and in their own time.

Some multiples also find psychodrama workshops to be helpful in processing some of their pain. Once again, these need to be facilitated by licensed professionals who are trained in childhood trauma and in multiplicity. Psychodrama can be a terrifying experience, and could even be dangerous in the hands of an amateur or professional who doesn't understand multiplicity well.

Making collages, drawing, painting, playing the piano, or baking bread can also be therapeutic activities. Any activity that is creative and helps to raise the multiple's self-esteem is worthwhile. Sometimes she/he may wish to perform these activities alone and other times may want you to share in the process. Many alters may take part, which gives you a chance to get to know all the different parts of the self.

Many multiples keep a journal in which all members of the system can write. This journal is *PRIVATE*. Do not ever peek into the journal unless specifically invited! Multiples are extremely protective of their privacy and of their boundaries. It is vital to respect this at all times.

A number of excellent survivor publications are on the market, many dealing specifically with multiplicity. Many multiples even read some of the clinical literature, finding that these books help to confirm their own truth about their condition. Reading these books and magazines may be helpful for you, too.

Support can also be found for the multiple, and for significant others, on computer bulletin boards such as Prodigy or Genie. A word of caution, however. Computer bulletin boards are open to the public and may be used by some cult members to trigger multiples into returning to cult behavior. Trust your instincts here.

Speaking from a personal standpoint, I found massage therapy to be extremely helpful in owning my own body and the things that happened to it. It is only through massage therapy that my body became mine. It is vital, however, that the massage therapist be chosen carefully. But don't push the issue. Many multiples and survivors of trauma simply don't want their bodies touched, and this need should be respected.

Any support, information, or publication that is meant for the multiple can also be a valuable tool for you as well. Read the literature, keep an open mind, and trust the multiple to do the best she/he can do with the resources available.

Depending on your relationship with the multiple, you may be asked to attend some therapy sessions. If you live together, it is important that you become a part of the multiple's healing.

Don't expect the multiple to share with you every memory or every trauma. Curb your curiosity and allow the multiple the dignity of choice. If she/he wants you to know, she/he'll tell you.

PRIVACY IS PRECIOUS.

Just as therapy is important for the multiple, therapy may be helpful for you as well. Living or working with a multiple can be stressful, and sometimes it helps to have the opinions and suggestions of a third party. Whether or not you see the same therapist is controversial and needs to be worked out between you.

Therapy is discussed in great detail in the following clinical books:

Diagnosis and Treatment of Multiple Personality Disorder
by Dr. Frank Putnam

Multiple Personality Disorder, Diagnosis, Clinical Features and Treatment
by Dr. Colin Ross

Treatment Of Adult Survivors Of Childhood Abuse
by Dr. Eliana Gil

MONEY

Where does the money go?

If you think this question confounds a singleton, try multiplying it by the number of alters in a multiple's system!

Just as there are differences in other aspects of a multiple's life, there will be differences in how each personality handles money.

One alter may be a penny pincher who saves every scrap of yarn and recycles the underwear. Another may be a compulsive spender who buys whatever she/he wants, with no thought of whether or not the money is available.

Checking accounts, credit cards, and mail order catalogs can be the most difficult to control. Savings accounts, and the "pin money" stashed in the fake cabbage may be reduced as different alters dip into the till.

Alters will sometimes buy things none of the others use. Jessica likes red wigs, Marta likes hats, the kids like toys, and Regina likes rock music. It is common for multiples to find items in the closet or around the house that nobody remembers buying or using.

How can you keep everybody happy without running up the equivalent of the National Debt?

In addition to agreements the multiple makes within their own system, you can make separate agreement with individual alters. Talk to one of the adults and gain their cooperation in keeping a lid on the spending practices of the others.

Unless you have money to burn, $300 phone bills and the purchase of fur coats are probably not in your budget. Just remember that when you make an agreement with the host or alters, do so in a reasonable manner.

Laying down the law or threatening retaliation will not achieve the desired result—but will probably produce more spending, more buying, and more hiding the evidence of purchases.

Be prepared for the fact that slips will occur. Not everybody in the system may agree to abide by the new rules, or may spend the money in active rebellion. Remain calm, and once again try to gain the cooperation of the system.

Remember that the abuse of money is as much a cry for help as a slit wrist. Alters within an individual system may have little or no experience in self-discipline, so it's important for you not to overreact.

To my knowledge, no book or pamphlet exists on dealing with the issue of money as it relates to multiples or survivors. A good credit counselor may have some insight as to basic spending and saving practices that the alters may agree to implement. Do not expect a "debt rescue" type organization to fulfill this need. Good credit counselors are usually a nonprofit, community service organization.

MEMORIES

Memories don't always come in the therapist's office. Sometimes they happen out in public or at work or in the privacy of your bedroom. They are terrifying, confusing, and produce anxiety, shame, and fear.

Sharing these memories is one of the most difficult things any multiple can do.

And listening to them may be one of the hardest things for you.

Whether or not you are privy to the memories the host or alters hold depends greatly on your relationship. If you are the multiple's partner, then it is possible that you will hear some pretty horrific stuff. If you're the boss, coworker or friend, or if you know the multiple in a more professional setting, then you may not know any of the details of his or her past.

Memories seem to come in three stages: Stage one is the memory itself. It may be fuzzy and indistinct, or sharp and painfully clear. It may take the form of a picture inside the head, a smell, a sound, a body memory, or just a sudden knowing.

Stage two is the denial of the memory. Denial is built right into the system. Denial helps to take the edge off the memory and gives the psyche a chance to get used to the truth.

Stage three is the acceptance of the memory. After the initial acceptance may come a flood of relief as the multiple realizes that she/he has one more puzzle piece of the past.

Many multiples fluctuate between stages two and three with the same memory for a long time.

What can you do if you are present when a memory surfaces?

You need to talk about choices and alternatives before the situation arises. Some alters may want to be held and comforted while remembering scenes of abuse. Others do not want to be touched at all, and still others may lash out at you in fear if you attempt to touch them.

Always, always ask before touching a multiple, especially during times of remembering abuses.

It is possible that the multiple will want you to simply go away and leave them alone. Other times she/he may want you to stay, but not do or say anything. It is important that you ask at the time. Just be aware that the multiple may not even know what she/he wants or expects from you.

You might want to offer a favorite stuffed animal or other safety object. This item may change depending on which alter is currently out.

And sometimes the only thing you can do is listen.

These videos may be helpful in understanding multiplicity and survivors of child sexual abuse:

No More Secrets, The Effects Of Childhood Sexual Abuse On Adult Survivors

Multiple Personality, Putting Many Faces On Child Abuse by Dr. Margo Rivera

Both videos are available from Sidran Foundation.

MULTIPLES AS PARENTS AND CAREGIVERS

How do you tell your outside kids that their parent is a multiple?

Luckily, young children are resilient and often sympathetic to the misfortunes of others. An age-appropriate explanation is definitely in order.

Kids usually know anyway. Children are not nearly as fragile or as oblivious as we sometimes think they are. They know that their parent is often inconsistent and sometimes acts like a child or gets upset and afraid. They know their parent is more lenient when she likes to be called Maggie, for example, than when she wants to be called Mom.

Kids know. By explaining the condition to them in terms they can understand, you are only putting a label on something they already recognize as being different.

Explain to the child that their parent often seems to have different people inside, and sometimes these people don't know each other. Sometimes the people may not seem to know them!

Tell them that it's different from having an imaginary friend. An imaginary friend is an outside pretend friend, wheras the different parts that live inside are very real. An imaginary friend doesn't make you do things you don't remember doing later.

It's very important that the children understand that they are not the cause of the parent's multiplicity. Children tend to think that everything is their fault, so you must be very, very clear on this. Explain that this condition began long before they were born.

Because each multiple is different, it is difficult to generalize here about exactly what to say to the children. You can explain that sometimes the parent wants to be called by a different name. You can say that lots of people have this same condition, but that most people don't talk much about it, especially to kids.

You can talk a little bit about therapy and how the therapist is going to help the parent get better. If the children are involved in therapy, it's important they get the opportunity to ask the therapist questions in private.

Kids will want to know if the parent is ever going to get better, how long it will take, and what they should do when somebody "different" comes out. They will want to know if they can tell their friends or teachers. Your answers will depend on your own situation and on how the multiple's condition manifests itself.

Children want to know if their parent is crazy. It's important to share with them that the parent is *NOT* crazy, but developed this survival skill because somebody hurt them in the past and this is how they got through it. Kids understand pain.

Kids will want to know if multiplicity is catching. The answer, of course, is no, multiplicity is not contagious. But, sometimes people with multiple personalities have someone inside that might try to hurt them, and it's important that they tell you if this should happen.

Let the kids know that it's okay to be confused. Even grown-up people are often confused about multiple personalities. Let them know it's okay to ask questions, and that it's important for them to tell if an alter hurts them or hurts their feelings.

It's even okay for them to have a preference for someone inside and not to like other parts. But it's not okay to play these parts against each other, like getting one part to say you can go to a party, for example, when you know that's really not okay.

The hospitalization of a multiple is a trying time for the whole family. Let the kids know that it wasn't their fault, and that the hospital is a place where the multiple can get help.

It's vital that these outside kids have somebody they can talk to about this condition. They will need help with their fears and their questions. An occasional therapy session for them might be helpful.

An excellent book for you and your kids is

Multiple Personality Disorder (MPD) Explained For Kids by Barbara Boat and Gary Peterson.

It is available from:
The Childhood Trust
Program on Childhood Trauma and Maltreatment
Department of Psychiatry, CB 7160
University of North Carolina
Chapel Hill, NC 27599
Phone: 919-966-1760

CHILDREN AS MULTIPLES

A great deal of information is available for and about adult multiples. Unfortunately there is precious little written for or about child multiples. Nonoffending parents, teachers, foster parents, and even some therapists may be unclear about how to deal with a child who has multiple personalities.

Children exhibit their multiplicity in a variety of ways. They are changeable beyond the norm of most children. One minute, for example, they love tuna casserole, the next minute they spit it out or throw it on the floor, shrieking that they've always hated tuna casserole.

They may talk to themselves, often using different voices. Now most children do this occasionally in play, so simply using different voices is not necessarily an indicator of multiplicity.

Child multiples may not recognize playmates, teachers, or even family members. They may not recognize items that belong to them, or insist that the item belongs to someone else.

They may startle frequently as alters speak inside their head. There may be self-injurious behavior or violent behavior toward other children or animals.

What appears to be lying to adults may be the switching of one alter to another. For the child multiple, they aren't lying. Alter Susie may do something, then retreat to let host Debbie take the blame. The trouble is that "Debbie" hasn't got a clue as to why she's in trouble and will protest mightily that she isn't guilty. Which she isn't.

Child multiples may become very upset when other outside children are disciplined. They may run and hide, scream, cry, or become very still and almost trancelike. Rapid switching may occur, as each alter sees the situation and then runs away.

A child multiple may have trouble making and keeping friends. A best friend can become a worst enemy, depending on which alter is out, and other children simply don't know how to handle the changes.

They may be afraid of certain places, the bathroom being fairly high on the list. They often don't want to be touched and may switch immediately if startled.

In school child multiples may deny their own work, their own drawings, and even refuse to sit in their own seat, stating that "I don't sit there, Harry does!" They may seem to be off in another world, or daydreaming. They may use both hands to write or draw and get confused easily.

One alter may know a subject extremely well, while another may not know anything at all about it. An "A" on a math test for one alter, may easily be an "F" for another.

Eyesight may change between the alters. One may be farsighted and another nearsighted. Talents may be different as well, with one alter being a singer, another a writer, and still another an artist.

Now comes the hard part—if your child is a multiple, and you are not the abuser, it is important to find out how and why your child became a multiple. You need to know if your child is still in danger, and if so, to get them out of danger.

The good news is that children with multiple personalities heal faster than adults when treatment is started early. Having a safe, supportive family is invaluable for a child multiple. Remove the danger and replace it with love and understanding. Get to know each part of the child, and let them all know they are loved and accepted. Have regular contact with your child's therapist. Establish firm but loving boundaries and discourage switching.

Discipline for a child multiple should never consist of corporal punishment, but may take the form of "time out" and restriction of certain privileges.

Teenage multiples present their own set of problems. In addition to normal teenage angst, the complications of multiplicity may make treatment difficult. If host Timmy gets arrested for holding up a liquor store when it was actually alter Marvin that did the crime, explaining multiplicity to law enforcement may be tricky.

Most teenagers are sometimes secretive and worried about whether their behavior or feelings are normal. Multiple teenagers experience the same feelings, except they also have lost time to deal with, besides being called a liar, or being punished for something another alter did.

Running away and suicide attempts are often seen in adolescent multiples.

As with young children, it is important that a teenage multiple feel accepted and loved. Insist on therapy, even if the teenager doesn't seem to be getting anything out of it. The sooner the multiple gets to the heart of the problem, the quicker the alters will begin to cooperate, and everybody can get on with their lives.

For a checklist on childhood multiple personality indicators, call:

Gwen L. Dean, Ph.D.
(310) 521-6659

and this book:

Growing Up Again, Parenting Ourselves, Parenting Our Children
by Jean Illsley Clarke, and Connie Dawson

MULTIPLES AS PATIENTS

If you are a doctor, dentist, anesthesiologist, opthalmologist, emergency medical technician, massage therapist, lab technician, or are otherwise affiliated with the medical community, dealing with a multiple may be puzzling and confusing even on your best days!

One of the hallmarks of multiplicity is that the multiple can change literally in the blink of an eye. Lab results will change from alter to alter. Eyesight can change from blindness to 20-20 vision, with all sorts of ranges in between. Evidence of broken bones may only appear on the x-rays of the personality who originally suffered the injury, and not when anyone else is out.

One personality may be allergic to penicillin or codeine, while none of the others are. Some may be allergic to certain foods or drinks, and the others not. One of Eve's personalities (*Three Faces Of Eve*), as I remember, was allergic to nylon, and her others were not.

Some personalities may show a positive pregnancy test, while others won't, even if the reality is that the body is pregnant. Male alters, for example, may test negative for pregnancy even if the body is pregnant.

Blood test results and even blood types can change from alter to alter. Medication reacts differently between the selves. An adult dose given to a child personality may cause severe reactions, while a child's dose taken may not be enough if the alter changes to an adult personality.

An anesthetic given to one personality may not filter over to the others, and your patient may awaken on the operating table.

A patient may come to see you with an illness or injury that none of the others have. Body memories may occur on the examining table, causing fear and panic, with you being mistaken for the perpetrator. Or receiving a massage may bring up long-buried memories and trauma.

Treating the physical ailments of a multiple patient can be tricky, but it can be done. Here are some hints to make your job a little easier:

1.   Whenever you are examining a multiple, especially if the procedure is invasive or painful, have a support person in the room. Sometimes just having someone there to hold her hand is enough to smooth over the embarrassment or apparent threat of the situation.

2.   Explain everything you are going to do before you do it. Tell the multiple how the procedure will feel and sound. Always give notice before touching the body. Explain each procedure thoroughly. Discuss side-effects of medications or procedures.

3.   Be aware that touching certain portions of the body may trigger a reaction. Most multiples are sensitive about their genital and rectal area, breasts, and mouth. Dentistry, including having X-rays taken, may be difficult for a multiple who was forced into oral sex, for example.

4.   Before beginning any procedure, be sure the personality with the problem is the one you are treating. If a switch occurs, stop and be sure that the new personality knows what is going on. Ask frequently if she/he is okay and get permission to continue.

5.   Before surgery that involves an anesthetic, you may need to make an agreement with the system that only one person will have the anesthetic, and that none of the others will come out during surgery. Explain procedures and side-effects beforehand.

6.   Multiples may need many pairs of glasses to accommodate the differences in eyesight.

7. Write down all instructions. Be sure your notes are clear and concise and easy enough for a child alter to understand. Avoid misunderstanding by writing the instructions yourself.

8. Medication should have childproof caps, even if there are no outside children in the house. Child alters can be suicidal sometimes, so it is important to have this safety measure in place. Prepare a chart for the refrigerator so the multiple's system can record when each medication was taken, and when the next dose is due. This added bit of caring will mean a great deal to a multiple.

9. Emergency room personel should be on the lookout for switching. Any situation that requires emergency care is going to be stressful for the whole system, so it is important to take extra care when working with a multiple.

10. Before the multiple leaves your office, be sure that an adult alter who knows how to drive home is in charge. If a child personality is out, ask for a responsible adult to drive home. It is usually best if the personality who came to the office is the same one to leave.

11. You might suggest that if any procedure seems scary, an adult personality take the children inside and tell them stories or otherwise keep them occupied. I wrote a couple of my best children's stories sitting in my dentist's chair.

12. Do not, under any circumstances, lie to the multiple! Don't, for example, say something is not going to hurt if it is. Multiples don't like surprises but would rather be prepared so that the system can handle whatever comes up.

I don't want to scare you into thinking that working with a multiple is going to be a traumatic experience for you. Most multiples manage quite well in a medical setting. Even if switches occur, just remember that the switch is for the benefit of the multiple's system and is probably better for you, too.

Just be certain that the multiple's system knows what you're doing every step of the way, and everything should be fine.

For more information on helping a multiple through the health care system, read:

Knowing The Ropes, How To Advocate Effectively For Consumers Of Psychiatric Services
Published by the Sidran Foundation and Mental Health Law Project.

MULTIPLES AT SCHOOL

GRADE SCHOOL CHILDREN

Young multiples may have a difficult time in school, especially if they are switching a lot in class or on the playground.

Teachers have reported children striking out at other children seemingly without provocation. In the case of a multiple, she/he may simply be reacting to being hit, kicked, or teased the last time she/he was out, because for them, there has been no lapse between the time of the occurrence and now.

We spoke before about some symptoms of switching; now let's talk about what you can do about it.

If you sense that a switch has occurred, don't make a big deal out of it. Give the class an assignment, then speak quietly to the multiple, giving him or her a little extra encouragement. Explain the assignment again, remembering that each personality may not have the same understanding of the subject matter.

New personalities may not even know who you are, or what grade they are in, especially if it has been some time since she/he was last out. She/he may not know anything at all about the subject, even if someone else in the system knows the subject backward and forward. Be patient.

Don't encourage a switch back to the original personality or to the one who knows the answers. This is real life, and each child needs to be able to function in the world, so everybody in the system needs to know the basics.

It is important not to make a show of singling this child out for special attention. Other children can be cruel and may pick on the child outside of the classroom or taunt the child as being "teacher's pet."

Keep your eyes and ears open for signs of current abuse. Children don't get to be multiples by living in Beaver Cleaver's house, so the safety of the child at home is of paramount importance.

Remember that you are a mandated reporter, so if you suspect that this child is still being abused, you must report this to the appropriate agencies.

JUNIOR HIGH AND HIGH SCHOOL CHILDREN

Because of the constant changing of classrooms in most junior and senior high schools, it may be difficult to spot a multiple or to see a switch. Personality Johnny may go to algebra, while Harriet goes to science, and Billy attends English class. Unless you teach in a one-room school, the only way you may know about a child's multiplicity is by comparing notes with other teachers.

It is important to remember that teenage multiples go through the same sorts of feelings and problems that nonmultiples go through. They have fights with their friends, get in trouble at home, are sweet and kind one minute, and throw their books across the room the next.

Nobody understands them. While this is a common cry from adolescents, in the multiple's case, it's very true. Their friends don't understand why the multiple doesn't remember an important conversation or a date. Teachers don't understand that one personality doesn't know anything that another personality does. Parents don't understand why their child switches from instant to instant.

Don't complain about time spent away from school to go to therapy. Make a little extra time after school to help with difficult assignments. If possible, ask the alters to share school information between them.

COLLEGE-AGE MULTIPLES

Adult multiples who attend college are amazing. These people can often take on a full load and get excellent grades, while holding down a full-time job and raising a family. One year, while I was attending college, I worked from 8:00AM until 5:00PM at my job, went to school from 6:00 to 10:00 each night, plus had a Saturday class, and was taking care of a husband and two children! I had a 3.5 grade point average.

Multiples usually like college because each alter has the opportunity to learn something about subjects that interest them.

It is rare to have problems with a multiple who attends college. Unless the system is dissociating frequently, with time loss and skipped classes being a difficulty, most multiples do extremely well. Grade-point average is generally high, and multiples usually excel in classes relating to psychology, child development, and children's literature.

If the subject matter of a lecture becomes distressing, however, it is possible that a switch will occur. In that case you must trust that the multiple's system itself will take care of the problem. By the time a multiple reaches adulthood, and therefore college age, a certain manner of living in the world is already in place.

Again, you may need to take a little extra time occasionally, just to make sure that everybody in the system knows the subject, but usually college-age multiples can take care of themselves pretty well.

For more information on working with children who have been abused, read:

The Silent Children, A Parent's Guide to the Prevention of Child Sexual Abuse
by Linda Tschirhart Sanford

MULTIPLES AS EMPLOYEES AND COWORKERS

If you have a multiple as an employee, you can consider yourself lucky. Multiples usually make excellent employees who work hard and bring a fresh, ever-changing perspective to the job. They usually arrive at work early and leave late.

They sometimes seem to do the work of ten people.

Actually, that's a pretty fair estimation of the kind of work a multiple can do. When one personality tires, another can take over. If one alter is uncomfortable performing one aspect of the job, a different one can step in. If a different perspective is needed for a problem, the multiple can usually provide it.

Are there problems? Of course there are. A multiple may need regular time off work to go to therapy. Occasionally she/he may switch at work and cause problems or not know the job sufficiently well to get it done. It is possible that the multiple may need some hospital time on occasion to deal with particularly traumatic memories. Body memories or a sudden flashback may send the multiple into a tailspin.

For the most part any multiple who is capable of working is more than capable of doing the job well. You can help by being supportive during difficult times. Don't complain about the time needed for therapy or the rare instance that she/he must go home due to a flashback. When the multiple is on the job, you're getting the work of ten people, so don't begrudge them the small amount of time they need to get better.

Many multiples work in the helping professions as nurses, lay counselors, rape crisis advocates, child care workers, or massage therapists; even as doctors or therapists! These people are usually supportive, kind, and excellent at working with people in crisis. For the most part, they need little or no supervision.

But what can you do when a problem does occur? Here are some tips that can help both you and the multiple weather a storm at work:

1. First of all, sometimes switching at work is a good thing. You can get a fresh point of view for some problem or situation or simply the energy that a new personality can provide. But if the alter who appears is behaving inappropriately, it is perfectly acceptable to ask for a different personality.

2. A teenage alter does not have the right to come out and swear at customers. A child alter shouldn't be working the computer. The system needs to know what the ground rules are and that you are prepared to enforce them.

3. For most multiples keeping their job is vital. Suggest that she/he gets their therapist to make an agreement with the alters so that only certain personalities come out at work or at business functions.

4. If the problem is a flashback or body memory, then a few minutes break is a good idea. You may need to allow a phone call to a support person, or let the person take time off work to go home. Multiples at work rarely allow memories to slow them down, so this problem should occur rarely, if at all.

5. Keep the workplace as safe and pleasant as possible. That's just good business sense any time. Do not allow sexual harassment of any kind. If the multiple is doing the harassing, explain in no uncertain terms that this behavior will not be tolerated.

Multiples need their jobs. They need money to support themselves and their families. They need insurance to afford therapy. They need the self-confidence and self-esteem that working every day brings.

A word of caution, however. Just because a multiple can work like ten people doesn't mean they should. Avoid the temptation to overwork the multiple, as a multiple burns out just like anybody else. It just takes them longer.

A multiple is usually an excellent employee, and you get the benefit of having lots of employees rolled up into one paycheck. Heck of a bargain, if you ask me.

MULTIPLES AS EMPLOYERS

The very same attributes that make a multiple a good employee may make a multiple a frustrating person to work for. If the multiple you know is your boss, then you probably walk a very fine line every day.

I once worked for a woman whom I am now convinced was a multiple. At the time, not knowing anything about my own multiplicity, I put her behavior down to mood swings, or even manic-depressive disorder.

This woman would send me flowers at work, telling me what a great job I was doing, and ten minutes later call me on the carpet for something she had praised me for doing earlier.

One of her alters was generous to a fault, and another was rigid and uncompromising. She would take us all out to a steak-and-lobster lunch, then chew us out when we returned for coming back late!

I really liked that job, but I just couldn't put up with her behavior. I told people at the time that it was "hard to work for somebody who's crazier than you are." Now, of course, I realize that she was switching from minute to minute, and each person in her system had a different idea of how to run the place.

It *IS* difficult to work for someone who changes their mind every time a new alter takes control. It's frustrating to be told how to do something one minute, then get chewed out for doing it that way. It's more than a little confusing to never be sure if you're doing your job the way the boss expects it to be done, when the boss changes her mind every time a switch occurs.

If your boss knows about her multiplicity, then working may be easier. The multiple may already have an agreement within the system about who goes to work. But if your boss doesn't know about the multiple personalities, working for this person can be a nightmare.

Remember that you have rights. You certainly have the right to complain if you are being treated unfairly. You have the right to quit your job and the right to stay and tough it out. You can take your complaints up the chain of command, but if the multiple is the highest rung on the ladder, then this doesn't do much good.

Working for a multiple, with all of its frustrations, can also be the perfect opportunity for you to work on your own issues of patience and compassion.

An excellent survivor's story that illustrates just how multiples deal with work, school, and life is:

The Flock, The Autobiography Of A Multiple Personality
by Joan Frances Casey, with Lynn Wilson

RITUAL AND CULT ABUSE

WARNING:

Some of this material may be upsetting. Much of it is graphic and distressing. If you are a survivor of incest or ritual abuse yourself, the information being presented may trigger certain emotional responses. You may find yourself getting extremely uncomfortable or dissociative. You may experience body pain, headache, or nausea. Feel free to skip this chapter if this is too distressing for you.

When an adult or child is abused in a ritualized manner, we use the term "ritual abuse." This may be done as part of a satanic or occult ritual; as part of an organized, fundamental belief system; by an individual; or by a group experimenting with the occult. Not all ritual abuse is satanic.

It is also important to note that not all people with multiple personalities are survivors of ritual abuse, just as not all ritual abuse survivors become multiples.

Ritual abuse memories, because they are the most horrific, are often the last to surface and are the most difficult to deal with. I´ you live with a ritual abuse survivor, you need a basic understanding of what the multiple you know went through.

Ritual abuse survivors report being abducted, abused, then returned; abused by their own cult families; abused in preschools; or by neighbors. As crazy as it may seem, sometimes this abuse may go on for years with no one suspecting.

One common myth is that children don't tell. Children and adults *do* tell, but sometimes the signs and symptoms are difficult to detect.

Children tell in a variety of ways, some overt and some covert. They tell by their behavior either by compulsively being drawn to particular activities or behaviors or by just as compulsively avoiding them.

Child alters may call certain items by descriptive terms rather than by their names, such as a "dead box" for a coffin or a "long dress" for the robes a cult member may wear.

They may be frightened or drawn to certain colors, usually red, black, or purple. They may be revolted by red meat, for example, because they may have been forced to consume human body parts during rituals. They may just as compulsively avoid red drinks, like tomato juice or Kool-Aid, because they may have been forced to drink blood during rituals. Cream drinks may also cause gagging and nausea, due to being forced to swallow semen.

Adult ritual abuse survivors may have suffered years of abuse, torture, and programming. Sometimes the abuse occurred within their own families. Much of this information is lost to the conscious memory, and what memories exist are fuzzy at best. Some of this is due to dissociating during the experiences, and some is due to programming by the cult.

Some cults deliberately try to create multiple personalities in their victims in order to have more power over them, or so that the level of abuse the person can take will increase as each alter comes out to take the pain.

Being forced to consume human feces or urine is common, with the result that toileting behavior and lack of personal hygiene may become an issue, especially with children.

Sometimes the child is "sold" into prostitution or pornography in order to create income for the cult. A multiple who was forced into prostitution as a child may have a prostitute alter as an adult. There may be a fear of cameras, especially video cameras.

The commercialization of children through the use of child pornography and prostitution is an 8.5 billion dollar industry in this country. One of the most disturbing facts of this business is that there is a market for it, which indicates a major flaw in the very fabric of our moral society.

Documentation of the abuse, such as still photographs or video images, can be used to blackmail the victim, or to exert control or influence over future behavior. It can be used to buy silence, especially if the victim/participant is a prominent member of the community. It also extends the brainwashing that the victim actually believes that she/he was a willing participant.

Pornography films are often professionally produced, and many children can be involved. Sometimes these children are housed like cattle, in inhumane conditions. The films range from simple nude pictures, to sex with adults and animals, to "snuff" films in which the child is actually murdered.

The whole point of ritual abuse is to gain control over the child, over his or her mind, heart, sexuality, and spirituality. It takes a strong person to resist this ancient programming.

Children are threatened in a variety of ways, sometimes by examples of what could happen to them if they tell. A favorite pet may be killed in front of them, for example, or pictures may be shown to them of mutilated bodies, with the explicit warning that if they tell, this will happen to them or someone they love.

Children of the cult are sometimes murdered in front of other children to prove the seriousness of the threats.

In some instances the child is made to commit a murder, so that the cult will have more power over them. "See," they will say, "you are one of us now," and "you can't ever tell or you will go to jail." They are made to believe that they committed the murder of their own free will, when threat and force took away any will of their own long since.

Self-mutilation and suicide attempts may mar a survivor's life, especially when the memories begin to surface.

In abuse that occurs outside the family, the child does not tell the parents because of fear of not being believed or the belief that they are saving the parents from harm. With abuse that happens in the family, the child is usually programmed that they will not be believed, and will be killed if they tell.

Brainwashing is systematic misinformation fed to the victim. Sometimes certain triggers are placed in the victims' mind to make them available for recontact at a later date by the cult, or "killing" triggers are placed so that the victim is programmed either to kill someone else or themselves if the "secret" is told.

A typical brainwashing technique is to perpetuate horrendous abuse on the child, then "rescue" the child from that same abuse. The child becomes confused and does not know who or what to believe or trust. Developing multiple personalities is a safe way out of the dilemma.

Sometimes the abuse is so horrific that denial will shift from the victim, to the significant others, to the therapist and back again during the whole therapy process. It is important to remain supportive and safe, even when your mind does not want to believe the events being related.

Working or living with "destructive" alters or with personalities who are still actively involved with the cult is difficult. Sexual activity may turn from a pleasant, gentle experience to a perverted, sordid activity with the switch of an alter.

Alters who are currently active in the cult may be secretive and unresponsive to therapy. She/he may disappear for days at a time, and you may find evidence of cult involvement. She/he may draw occult symbols or may have a "stash" of curved-handled knives, chalices, or ceremonial robes in purple, red, or black.

Personal appearance can become a nightmare for a ritual abuse survivor. Looking nice means you get hurt. Dressing in fancy clothes means you get hurt. Bathing and being clean means you get hurt. It becomes "bad" to have nice things, because the victim believes these things are bought with the blood of innocents.

It may help significant others to know what triggers may cause distress or switching. A trigger, in this case, is something that indicates that cult programming is starting to take hold.

Some of these include: Headache; numbness of the extremities or the mouth; blurred vision; ringing in the ears; a bad taste in the mouth (like feces, for example); a feeling of being watched or tied up; pain; hyperventilation; feeling faint or dizzy; sleepiness; compulsive activities or impulses; a person known to be safe suddenly feels "evil"; extreme terror for no apparent reason; joint pain; vomiting; unconsciousness.

Other triggers include: certain colors, especially red, black, and purple; certain jewelry like pentagrams, crosses, animal shapes, or feathers, and the "horned" hand; small, dark places; occult material or literature; certain phrases, words, or statements; use of ritual-oriented activities; stuffed animals, especially rabbits; certain cologne or perfume or alcohol smells; cameras, videotaping, or tape recording; drawings of hearts; uniformed people; abstract images; and numbers.

Once the triggers have been activated, there are certain indications that current victimization is taking place. They include repeated harassment by family, friends, or strangers; harassing phone calls; "night sounds" like whistles, drums, or horns; the delivery of dead animals, feces, urine, blood or body parts; or a sense of being followed. Criminal activity, (vandalism, burglary or theft, or physical or sexual assault), either perpetuated or attempted, may be an attempt by the cult to regain contact.

A multiple may experience unexplained bruising or injury; puncture wounds; drugged states, self-mutilation; blood on self or others; disclosure of recent abuse; and repeated unasked-for advice from therapists or significant others.

If the multiple you know is experiencing any of these symptoms, it is important to seek professional help right away. Don't try to deal with the situation by yourself. Cult people are dangerous and not taking these signs seriously could be hazardous or even fatal for you or for the multiple you care about.

Luckily, there is now a fair amount of material written about and for ritual abuse survivors. You may find the following material helpful:

Out Of Darkness, Exploring Satanism And Ritual Abuse
Edited by David K. Sakheim, Ph.D., and Susan E. Devine, R.N., M.S.N.

Suffer The Child
by Judith Spencer (this book is graphic and riveting, not for the faint-hearted.)

and this video:

Children At Risk
produced by Cavalcade Productions, available from Sidran Foundation.

TAKING CARE OF YOURSELF

Having any kind of relationship with a multiple can be exhilarating, exciting, frustrating, confusing, and draining. It is easy to become overwhelmed, especially if you are a friend or partner.

This may be the most important statement I make in this entire book:

YOU NEED TO TAKE CARE OF YOURSELF— FIRST!

Yes—your friend or your partner may be going through difficult times. Yes—it's hard to say no when she/he is in crisis. And yes—you are important to the multiple's healing.

But you aren't going to do the multiple any good if you allow yourself to become burned out. You can't save him or her, you can't fix it, and you can't make the child abuse that caused the multiplicity go away.

What you can do is be a good friend. Treat the multiple with respect and with care. Be honest and be available as much as possible. Do fun things together. It's okay to enjoy each other's company, as well as be there during the hard times.

But you also need to take care of yourself. It's okay to say no when you're not feeling up to listening or to say no to other requests if you feel uncomfortable or unable to respond.

When you are listening, or providing care and comfort, remember to stay focused in the present. It's not the past events she/he is relating that are important but rather the current feelings that are affecting their daily life.

It is easy to become so involved with the multiple's pain that you take it on yourself. You need to keep your self separate and not allow the horror of the multiple's experiences to cloud your own perceptions of current reality.

Take time for yourself to do things you enjoy. It may mean long baths or short jogs; hot fudge sundaes with an old friend or a good massage. Treat yourself to some quiet time alone every day. Meditate. Keep yourself healthy. Eat right and get plenty of rest.

The multiple you know is probably a warm, wonderful, caring person. She/he has trusted you with the truth about his or her condition, and you have responded with care and concern by reading this book.

For me, and for the multiple you know, I say thank you for being a friend and for caring.

SPEAKING FOR THEMSELVES

When I was researching the material for this book, I interviewed a number of multiples and asked the question, "What do you want your significant others to know about you?"

The most overwhelming reply was, "I want them to know I'm not crazy!"

The following replies have been paraphrased, condensed, and/or combined so as not to betray identity:

- I don't look like myself.

- How can I believe it when you say I'm beautiful, when I look in the mirror and only see ugliness?

- Don't argue with argumentative alters.

- Please help me keep my biological kids safe!

- I don't want my boss to know anything. I could lose my job.

- I write all my appointments on the calendar so everybody will know where we need to be and when.

- Tell the doctors that we really need to be listened to. We aren't trying to be difficult; it's just that some of us are scared.

- Being hospitalized is not necessarily a sign of weakness or insanity. It's a sign of strength when we recognize that we need the extra protection.

- I'm not a murderer. That's only in the movies.

- Don't try to control me or my behavior or my alters. How are we ever going to learn to control ourselves if you do it for us?

- Tell my outside kids that I don't mean to hurt them.

- I wish my partner would respect my wishes when I don't want to be touched.

- I don't have False Memory Syndrome!

- Please believe me when I tell you the things that happened to me. This stuff hurts too much to make up.

- I'm not just moody. This is real.

- Sometimes I'm afraid and I don't know why.

- I don't expect you to fix it.

- If I was physically ill, with pneumonia or cancer or something, the boss would let me take the time off I needed to go to the doctor. Well, my therapy is just as important as that.

- I'm still the same person I always was. Having a label to put on my behavior doesn't make me different.

- Don't tell me to snap out of it!

- I'm not a freak or a sideshow attraction. Don't watch me every minute for switching.

- Multiplicity is not like the flu. You can't catch it from me.

- I know I don't act like the people in the movies. I'm still a multiple.

- When you're talking to me, remember that the others are listening, too.

- Thank you for not running away. You don't know how much it means to have you stay, even when we act strange. I know how difficult it must be for you. And I know how hard it is to hear about the things that happened to me.

I also asked some significant others what advice they would have to give to others, and this is what they said (also paraphrased, condensed and/or combined):

- You can't fix it for them.

- Don't try to be their therapist.

- Read about multiplicity so you will understand what you're seeing, and so you can help if the therapist is unavailable.

- Sometimes they push you away because it feels safer for them.

- Don't allow yourself to be abused. It's okay to say, "I don't deserve to be treated like this."

- Learn to ask. Don't assume.

- Always ask their permission to touch. And don't get upset if that permission is denied.

- Never lie to a multiple.

- Play fair. Don't tease or make jokes about their condition.

- Sometimes you have to run block for them with the health care system. Don't let doctors or nurses or hospitals take advantage of them.

- Stay out of his or her "safe" place, and don't read their diary!

- I don't let my partner read the ritual abuse literature. We don't want her own memories contaminated by something she read.

- Find out what makes the multiple feel safe. Then do it.

- I had to shave my beard, because a scratchy face scared the kids.

- If you don't listen to the alters, they can make life really miserable trying to get your attention.

- Be consistent.

- It's okay to get help for yourself. Learn ways to take care of yourself. It's okay not to be there for him or her every second.

- Don't talk about the multiple's condition or progress with outsiders. Maintain confidentiality.

- Be patient. Abuse severe enough to cause multiple personalities is not going to be "cured" over night.

- Ask "What do you want to tell me?", not "Tell me everything."

- You're not going to like everybody in the system, and not everybody is going to like you.

- It's not their fault.

- It gets better. Honest it does. Just hang in there, and things get better.

Another survivor's story you may find helpful is:

When Rabbit Howls
By The Troops for Truddi Chase

m8096tN
19